AMAZING ANIMALS
OF THE WORLD ②

Volume 1

Adder — Buffalo, Water

GROLIER

First published 2005 by Grolier, an imprint of Scholastic Library Publishing

© 2005 Scholastic Library Publishing

For information address the publisher: Grolier, Scholastic Library Publishing
90 Old Sherman Turnpike
Danbury, CT 06816

Set ISBN: 0-7172-6112-3; Volume ISBN: 0-7172-6113-1

Printed and bound in the U.S.A.

Library of Congress Cataloging-in-Publications Data:
Amazing animals of the world 2.
p.cm.
Includes indexes.
Contents: v. 1. Adder—Buffalo, Water -- v. 2. Bunting, Corn—Cricket, Bush -- v. 3. Cricket, European Mole—Frog, Agile -- v. 4. Frog, Burrowing Tree—Guenon, Moustached -- v. 5. Gull, Great Black-backed—Loach, Stone -- v. 6. Locust, Migratory—Newt, Crested -- v. 7. Nuthatch, Eurasian—Razor, Pod -- v. 8. Reedbuck, Mountain—Snake, Tentacled -- v. 9. Snakefly—Toad, Surinam -- v. 10. Tortoise, Gopher—Zebu.
ISBN 0-7172-6112-3 (set : alk. paper) -- ISBN 0-7172-6113-1 (v. 1 : alk. paper) -- ISBN 0-7172-6114-X (v. 2 : alk. paper) -- ISBN 0-7172-6115-8 (v. 3 : alk. paper) -- ISBN 0-7172-6116-6 (v. 4 : alk. paper) -- ISBN 0-7172-6117-4 (v. 5 : alk. paper) -- ISBN 0-7172-6118-2 (v. 6 : alk. paper) -- ISBN 0-7172-6119-0 (v. 7 : alk. paper) -- ISBN 0-7172-6120-4 (v. 8 : alk. paper) -- ISBN 0-7172-6121-2 (v. 9 : alk. paper) -- ISBN 0-7172-6122-0 (v. 10 : alk.paper)
1. Animals--Juvenile literature. I. Title: Amazing animals of the world two. II. Grolier (Firm)
QL49.A455 2005
590--dc22
                                                                                    2005040351

About This Set

Amazing Animals of the World 2 brings you pictures of 400 fascinating creatures and important information about how and where they live.

Each page shows just one species—individual type—of animal. They all fall into seven main categories or groups of animals (classes and phylums scientifically) that appear on each page as an icon or picture—amphibians, arthropods, birds, fish, mammals, other invertebrates, and reptiles. Short explanations of what these group names mean, and other terms used commonly in the set, appear on page 4 in the Glossary.

Scientists use all kinds of groupings to help them sort out the thousands of types of animals that exist today and once wandered here (extinct species). Kingdoms, classes, phylums, genus, and species are among the key words here that are also explained in the Glossary (page 4).

Where animals live is important to know as well. Each of the species in this set lives in a particular place in the world, which you can see outlined on the map on each page. And in those locales the animals tend to favor a particular habitat—an environment the animal finds suitable for life, with food, shelter, and safety from predators that might eat it. There they also find ways to coexist with other animals in the area that might eat somewhat different food, use different homes, and so on. Each of the main habitats is named on the page and given an icon/picture to help you envision it. The habitat names are further defined in the Glossary on page 4.

As well as being part of groups like species, animals fall into other categories that help us understand their lives or behavior. You will find these categories in the Glossary on page 4, where you will learn about carnivores, herbivores, and other types of animals.

And there is more information you might want about an animal—its size, diet, where it lives, and how it carries on its species—the way it creates its young. All these facts and more appear in the data boxes at the top of each page.

Finally, you should know that the set is arranged alphabetically by the most common name of the species. That puts most beetles, say, together in a group so you can compare them easily.

But some animals' names are not so common, and they don't appear near others like them. For instance, the chamois is a kind of goat or antelope. To find animals that are similar—or to locate any species—look in the index at the end of each book in the set (pages 45-48). It lists all animals by their various names (you will find the giant South American river turtle under turtle, giant South American river, and also under its other name—arrau). And you will find all birds, fish, and so on gathered under their broader groupings.

Similarly, smaller like groups appear in the set index as well—butterflies include swallowtails and blues, for example.

Table of Contents
Volume 1

Glossary

Amphibians—species usually born from eggs in water or wet places, which change (metamorphose) into a land animal. Frogs and salamanders are typical. They breathe through their skin mainly and have no scales.

Arctic and Antarctic—icy, cold, dry areas at the ends of the globe that lack trees but see small plants grown in thawed areas (tundra). Penguins and seals are common inhabitants.

Arthropods—animals with segmented bodies, hard outer skin, and jointed legs, such as spiders and crabs.

Birds—born from eggs, these creatures have wings and often can fly. Eagles, pigeons, and penguins are all birds, though penguins can't fly through the air.

Carnivores—they are animals that eat other animals. Many species do eat each other sometimes, and a few eat dead animals. Lions kill their prey and eat it, while vultures clean up dead bodies of animals.

Cities, Towns, and Farms—places where people live and have built or used the land and share it with many species. Sometimes these animals live in human homes or just nearby.

Class—part or division of a phylum.

Deserts—dry, often warm areas where animals often are more active on cooler nights or near water sources. Owls, scorpions, and jack rabbits are common in American deserts.

Endangered—some animals in this set are marked as endangered because it is possible they will become extinct soon.

Extinct—these species have died out altogether for whatever reason.

Family—part of an order.

Fish—water animals (aquatic) that typically are born from eggs and breathe through gills. Trout and eels are fish, though whales and dolphins are not (they are mammals).

Forests and Mountains—places where evergreen (coniferous) and leaf-shedding (deciduous) trees are common, or that rise in elevation to make cool, separate habitats. **Rainforests are different (see below).**

Fresh Water—lakes, rivers, and the like carry fresh water (unlike Oceans and Shores, where the water is salty). Fish and birds abound, as do insects, frogs, and mammals.

Genus—part of a family.

Grasslands—habitats with few trees and light rainfall. Grasslands often lie between forests and deserts, and they are home to birds, coyotes, antelope, and snakes, as well as many other kinds of animals.

Herbivores—these animals eat mainly plants. Typical are hoofed animals (ungulates) that are common on grasslands, such as antelope or deer. Domestic (nonwild) ones are cows and horses.

Hibernators—species that live in harsh areas with very cold winters slow down their functions then and sort of sleep through the hard times.

Kingdom—the largest division of species. Commonly there are understood to be five kingdoms: animals, plants, fungi, protists, and monerans.

Mammals—these creatures usually bear live young and feed them on milk from the mother. A few lay eggs (monotremes like the platypus) or nurse young in a pouch (marsupials like opossums and kangaroos).

Migrators—some species spend different seasons in different places, moving to where more food, warmth, or safety can be found. Birds often do this, sometimes over long distances, but others types of animals also move seasonally, including fish and mammals.

Oceans and Shores—seawater is salty, often deep, and huge. In it live many fish, invertebrates, and even some mammals, such as whales. On the shore birds and other creatures often gather.

Order—part of a class.

Other Invertebrates—animals that lack backbones or internal skeletons. Many, such as insects and shrimp, have hard outer coverings. Clams and worms are also invertebrates.

Phylum—part of a kingdom.

Rainforests—here huge trees grow among many other plants helped by the warm, wet environment. Thousands of species of animals also live in these rich habitats.

Reptiles—these species have scales, lungs to breathe, and lay eggs or give birth to live young. Dinosaurs are thought to have been reptiles, while today the class includes turtles, snakes, lizards, and crocodiles.

Scientific name—the genus and species name of a creature in Latin. For instance, Canis lupus is the wolf. Scientific names avoid the confusion possible with common names in any one language or across languages.

Species—a group of the same type of living thing. Part of an order.

Subspecies—a variant but quite similar part of a species.

Territorial—many animals mark out and defend a patch of ground as their home area. Birds and mammals may call quite small or quite large spots their territories.

Vertebrates—animals with backbones and skeletons under their skins

Adder
Vipera berus

Length: 25 inches
Diet: small mammals, amphibians, and other reptiles

Number of Eggs: 3 to 20
Home: Europe and Asia
Order: Snakes
Family: Vipers

 Forests and Mountains

 Reptiles

© GEORGE MCCARTHY / CORBIS

The adder is one of Europe's most familiar snakes. Ancient priests, called Druids, believed that these snakes produced small magical objects known as adder stones. These stones were supposed to hold some of the adder's spirit. Many superstitious people believed that an adder stone could help them solve a legal problem or cure a sickness. In reality, adder stones are just smooth, round rocks.

Another myth is that you can coax an adder to drink from a bowl of milk. This would be quite difficult to do, however, since adders avoid humans whenever possible. They stay hidden for much of the day and come out at night to hunt. Still, sometimes it's hard not to trip over one of these common snakes. Once, English farm workers discovered 2,400 adders on a single acre of land!

Adders are vipers, and, like all vipers, they are poisonous. An adder bite will usually cause swelling, pain, vomiting, and dizziness. In some cases, it can even kill a person. Normally, the adder uses its poison to kill its prey—small animals such as lizards and baby birds.

Even before they hatch, baby adders have dangerous fangs. This is a potential hazard to the mother who is carrying them, because snake eggs have soft shells. To avoid an accident, nature has made sure that the fangs of the unborn adders are tucked down and away from the front end of the shell.

Rhombic Night Adder
Causus rhombeatus

Length: 16 to 40 inches
Diet: toad and small rodents
Home: central and southern Africa

Number of Eggs: 15 to 26
Order: Lizards and snakes
Family: Vipers

 Grasslands

 Reptiles

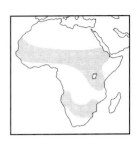

The rhombic night adder, like its American cousins the cottonmouth and the rattlesnake, has a poisonous bite. But the night adder rarely attacks humans. The snake's prey is much smaller—mainly mice, small gophers, and toads. When the adder opens its mouth to strike, its curved fangs swing forward, ready to deliver venom.

True to its name, the rhombic night adder is most active after dusk. It avoids the heat of the African sun by hiding under logs and rocks or burrowing inside termite mounds. The name "rhombic" comes from the dark blotches on the snake's back. These geometric marks are in the shape of a rhombus, a squarish figure with slanting sides. The rhombic night adder can also be recognized by a V-shaped mark on the top of its head.

Normally this snake moves slowly, as if half-asleep. But when disturbed, the night adder snaps to attention. It rises to face its attacker with its body inflated and its neck flattened broadly from side to side. Fortunately for careless humans, the rhombic night adder is not quick to strike. Instead, it hisses and huffs in a very threatening manner, allowing its foe to back away.

While many vipers give birth to live young, the rhombic night adder is an exception. It lays a large clutch of eggs in the summer, two full months before they will hatch.

Orange-rumped Agouti
Dasyprocta aguti

Length of the Body: 16 to 24 inches
Length of the Tail: ½ to 1 inch
Weight: 3½ to 8½ pounds
Diet: fruits and green plants

Number of Young: usually 2
Home: South America
Order: Rodents
Family: Agoutis

 Rainforests

Mammals

© JANY SAUVANET / PHOTO RESEARCHERS

The orange-rumped agouti is an oddly shaped rodent that lives in the warm, humid regions of South America. Unlike the relatively small North American rodents, the agouti can reach a length of 2 feet! Amazingly, this creature is dwarfed by its closest cousins, the pacas and capybaras of South America. The agouti's head and shoulders are much smaller than its plump hindquarters and large back legs. There are many species of agouti in the American tropics. Because they are similar in size and shape, they are generally identified by the color of their fur.

These creatures are solitary and live in separate territories. In the safety and serenity of the rainforest, agoutis are active during the day. They switch to a nocturnal lifestyle in areas where they are disturbed or hunted by humans. These nighttime rodents often make long trips outside their territories to fetch mangoes and other large fruits. Agoutis do not eat the fruits immediately. Instead, they hurry home with the fruit, where they carefully peel and eat it.

Males and females socialize only at mating time. Before giving birth, the female digs a series of cozy dens, each slightly larger than the last. As the babies outgrow the smallest den, the mother carries them to the next-larger one. This process continues for about four months, by which time the young agoutis are ready to dig their own burrows.

Alpaca
Lama pacos

Length: up to 3 feet
Height: 3½ to 4 feet
Weight: up to 150 pounds
Diet: grass and leaves
Number of Young: 1

Home: Andes Mountains of South America
Order: Even-toed hoofed animals
Family: Camels

 Forests and Mountains

Mammals

© RON WATTS / CORBIS

The alpaca lives high in the Andes Mountains of South America. It is among the smaller members of the camel family. But except for its long neck, the alpaca looks more like a large sheep. Its thick, silky wool, which ranges in color from white to brown to black, can grow to 2 feet in length. Some alpacas yield as much as 7 pounds of wool each year. The wool is used to make fine coats and other garments.

Three close relatives of the alpaca—the guanaco, the vicuna, and the llama—also live in the Andes. The guanaco and the vicuna are wild animals. The alpaca and the llama, however, were tamed by the Incas long before the Spanish conquered South America in the 1500s. Since that time, llamas have been raised for their meat and used as pack animals, just like mules. Alpacas, however, have been raised for their wool, just like sheep.

Alpacas live in large flocks. They graze on grass, and their wild relatives often graze with them. It is believed that the alpaca is descended from the guanaco. And it is not uncommon for alpacas and wild guanacos to crossbreed. Alpacas mate during the late summer and early fall. The young are born about 11 months later. They nurse for four to six months. They seem to be born frisky: within hours of birth, they are running and jumping around.

Opelet Anemone
Anemonia sp.

Width of the Disk: about 3 inches
Length of the Tentacles: up to 6 inches
Diet: mainly small fish, mollusks, and crustaceans

Methods of Reproduction: sexual or asexual
Home: Atlantic Ocean and Mediterranean Sea
Order: Sea anemones
Family: Actinarid anemones

 Oceans and Shores

 Other Invertebrates

© BIOPHOTO ASSOCIATES / PHOTO RESEARCHERS

Several species of large anemones are known commonly as opelets. They are recognized by their long, thin purplish tentacles. The name "opelet" is an Old English word meaning "open." Unlike other anemones, opelets cannot fully close their tentacles, which wave like long strands of grass. Although the tentacles are thin and fragile, they are powerful weapons. Do not touch! Opelets can deliver a painful sting.

The main purpose of the opelet's sting is to stun small fish and other prey animals. It then pulls the paralyzed fish to its mouth, at the top center of its round body. It digests food quickly and passes the waste material out through its mouth.

The anemone gets additional nutrition from algae, called zooxanthellae, which live in its tissues. The algae benefit as well, because the anemone provides them with a safe home. The algae give the anemone's body a greenish hue. Sometimes a lack of sunlight kills the algae. When this happens, the anemone turns white.

Opelet anemones that live off the shores of Europe attach themselves to rocks and other hard objects in shallow water. One species of opelet, *Anemonia sargassiensis*, lives in the Sargasso Sea in the western Atlantic Ocean. This creature remains attached to mats of floating seaweed, called sargasso weed.

Silver-spotted Anemone (Gem Anemone)
Bunodactis sp.

Length: about 1½ inches
Diet: plankton, dissolved animal matter, small fish, and crustaceans
Methods of Reproduction: egg layer and budding

Width: about 2 inches
Home: Mediterranean Sea and coastal waters of the northern Atlantic Ocean
Order: Sea anemones
Family: Endomyaria

 Oceans and Shores

Other Invertebrates

© ADRIAN DAVIES / BRUCE COLEMAN INC.

The small, colorful sea anemones in the genus *Bunodactis* are called gem anemones in Europe. In North America they are called silver-spotted anemones. Both common names refer to the glistening white spots on the anemone's tentacles. Anemones in this genus tend to be short and squat—noticeably wider than they are tall. Silver-spotted anemones can be found in various pastel colors, including olive green, blue, and pale red. Their stalks are crowned with a thick circle of long, stout tentacles.

Silver-spotted anemones live in shallow water, usually along sandy stretches of beach. Each anemone firmly attaches the suckerlike base of its body to a rock near the low-tide line. When the tide is at its lowest, many anemones are left out of the water for an hour or so. To keep from drying out in the open air, the anemone allows a thin layer of moist sand to cover its sticky skin.

The *Bunodactis* anemone seen along the coasts of Maine and Nova Scotia is an easily recognized species. It has six shiny white lines that extend outward from its central mouth like the spokes of a wheel. Each individual has a total of 120 tentacles. (The number of tentacles around a sea anemone's mouth is always a multiple of six.) Like all anemones the silver-spotted species can reproduce by either budding or spawning.

Anoa
Bubalus depressicornis

Length of the Body: about 6 feet
Length of the Tail: about 15 inches
Weight: up to 660 pounds
Diet: plants and herbs
Number of Young: 1

Home: island of Sulawesi in Indonesia
Order: Even-toed hoofed mammals
Family: Bovines
Subfamily: Cattle
Suborder: Ruminants

 Forests and Mountains

 Mammals

© KENNETH FINK / BRUCE COLEMAN INC.

? Endangered Animals

The anoa, or dwarf water buffalo, is the smallest and most ancient species of wild cattle in the world. But don't let its size fool you. This is a fierce and dangerous animal. If bothered, the irritable anoa is likely to attack, using its sharp horns as daggers. Despite this wild ox's fearsomeness, few people have reason to fear its attack because the anoa is found only on the Indonesian island of Sulawesi. Even there the animal is quite rare. The anoa is disappearing in part because the island is becoming crowded with people. In addition, many anoas die of infectious diseases and parasites. To make matters worse, they are often hunted for sport, and their horns and skin are considered valuable trophies.

Scientists believe that the anoa may never have lived beyond the shores of its small island, because its bones have not been found anywhere else. On Sulawesi, there are two types of anoa. The lowland anoa, *B. depressicornis*, lives in the moist woods on the north end of the island. The slightly smaller mountain anoa, *B. quarlesi*, lives in the mountains.

Because anoas are so rare, zoologists are working hard to breed them in captivity. But the task is difficult. They are quarrelsome and must be kept in separate enclosures except during mating season. They also become sick easily if not fed the proper diet.

Leaf-cutter Ant
Atta sexdens

Length: .4 to .6 inch (soldier); .08 to .35 inch (worker)
Diet: fungi
Method of Reproduction: egg layer

Home: Central America and South America
Order: Social insects
Family: Myrmicid ants

 Grasslands

 Arthropods

© MICHAEL & PATRICIA FOGDEN / CORBIS

Leaf-cutter ants are some of the most successful "farmers" of the insect world. They live in huge colonies, a single one containing as many as 8 million ants. Each member of the colony has a specific job. Some of the ants travel from the nest to nearby plants. They cut sections from leaves and carry the sections back to the nest. There other ants chew the leaves and place them in garden chambers. Drops of excrement are deposited on the leaves as fertilizer. A whitish fungus that looks like bread mold grows on the leaves.

The tiniest ants in the colony tend the fungus garden, transplanting bits of fungi from places where growth is too dense to places on newly chewed leaves. They also pick strands of fungi and carry them out of the garden to feed other members of the colony.

All the millions of members of the colony are children of the queen ant. Most of the ants are wingless females. These are the workers and soldiers. The few leaf-cutter ants that have wings are the males. The only females that have wings are the ones that become queens. The male's only purpose is to mate with the young queen; the male dies soon after mating. When a young queen leaves to form a new colony, she carries a bit of fungus. She finds an appropriate place for a nest, digs a chamber, and begins to lay eggs. She cultivates the fungus until the eggs hatch into workers, who can then take over the farming.

Dwarf Anteater
Cyclopes didactylus

Length of the Body: 6½ to 9 inches
Length of the Tail: 6½ to 12 inches
Weight: 10 to 17 ounces
Diet: mainly ants and termites

Number of Young: 1
Home: Central America and northern South America
Order: New World edentates
Family: Anteaters

 Rainforests

 Mammals

© JANY SAUVANET / PHOTO RESEARCHERS

The dwarf anteater is the smallest species of anteater. It is about the size of the common squirrel, with a tail as long as or longer than its body. The dwarf anteater is also called the silky anteater because of its soft, silky fur.

The creature lives in warm tropical forests, spending its entire life in trees. The kapok tree is the anteater's favorite home, because the animal's yellow-gray fur blends well with the tree's leaves. This camouflage makes it difficult for enemies such as owls, harpy eagles, snakes, and humans to spot the anteater.

During the day, dwarf anteaters sleep curled up in a tree hole or in the fork formed where two branches meet. But at night they make up for lost time, climbing tree trunks and crawling slowly along branches, looking for ants, termites, bees, and wasps. They use the powerful curved claws on their front feet to pick up prey and carry it to their mouth. Like all anteaters, dwarf anteaters have no teeth. Their long tongue—which looks like a worm—is covered with a sticky saliva. Dwarf anteaters have an excellent sense of smell, but not very good eyesight or hearing.

Both parents help raise the young anteater. At first the baby feeds only on its mother's milk. Later both parents feed it partly digested insects.

Scaly Anteater (Giant Pangolin)
Manis gigantea

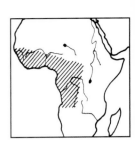

Length: to 6 feet
Weight: up to 70 pounds
Diet: termites and ants
Number of Young: 1 or 2

Home: tropical West Africa
Order: Pangolins
Family: Pangolins

 Grasslands

 Mammals

© KEREN SU / CORBIS

The giant pangolin is without a doubt one of the strangest mammals in the world. It has a very small head and short legs. Its long body is covered with large, overlapping scales moved by powerful muscles that can cause serious injury. The giant pangolin sits on its hind legs and large tail when it starts to attack an anthill or a termite mound. First, it scratches the ground with its front feet, which have large curved claws good for digging. As soon as the mound is opened, the giant pangolin dives into it and catches the insects that live there with its long sticky tongue. Its tongue can reach into all the little corners and does not seem to be bothered by the insects' stings.

The insects, panicked by this attack, try to escape. They climb by the thousands onto the pangolin, which keeps up its destructive work without worry. Why should it worry? Its eyes and nostrils can be closed off by thick membranes. Its body is protected by scales, which move up and down, crushing any insects that get under them.

This strange animal lives in humid parts of the forest and in savannas in western and central Africa. During the day, it hides in a large burrow that ends in a deep, underground room that's about 6 feet wide. It goes out at night to look for food. If the pangolin feels in danger, it curls up in a ball to protect its stomach, which does not have scales. It stays in this position so tightly that even several people cannot uncurl it.

Blue-spotted Argus
Cephalopholis argus

Length: about 12 inches
Diet: fish, crabs, crayfish, and other crustaceans
Method of Reproduction: egg layer

Weight: about 3 pounds
Home: Indo-Pacific seas
Order: Perchlike fishes
Family: Groupers

Oceans and Shores

Fish

© FRED MCCONNAUGHEY / PHOTO RESEARCHERS

A blue-spotted argus swimming against the background of a shady coral reef is nearly invisible. Like underwater chameleons, arguses camouflage themselves by producing spots and stripes in their skin. This fish undergoes a dramatic color change if it is wounded or taken from the water. It turns a brilliant blue when dying and fades to dull black when dead.

Blue-spotted arguses live solitary lives, each occupying a cave or crevice near the top of a coral reef. The fish seldom roams farther than 35 feet from its private hideaway. It is a skillful predator, with a mouth crammed with rows of needle-sharp, inward-slanting teeth. Once an argus sinks

its teeth into another fish, the prey has little hope of breaking free. The blue-spotted argus also has the amazing ability to stretch its mouth and stomach around fish just as large as itself! A typical foot-long blue-spotted argus often polishes off 8-inch-long parrotfish and goatfish with ease.

When approached by a diver or snorkeler, the blue-spotted argus always reacts one way: first it swims a short distance away. Then it suddenly turns to face the diver. There it hangs in the water, staring motionless for several seconds, a perfect target for the underwater photographer. The blue-spotted argus is easily caught with fishing lines, traps, and nets.

Common Backswimmer
Notonecta undulata

Length: ½ to ¾ inch
Diet: mosquito larvae, small crustaceans, insects, snails, and small fish
Home: North America

Method of Reproduction: egg layer
Order: True bugs
Family: Backswimmers

 Fresh Water

 Arthropods

© E. R. DEGGINGER / COLOR PIC. INC.

The common backswimmer is aptly named. This insect always swims on its back! It flips to an upright position only when it walks on dry land—something it rarely does. The backswimmer is easy to identify in the water. Any insect you see swimming on its back is sure to be either a common backswimmer or one of its close relatives. The common backswimmer can also be recognized by its extremely long hind legs, which the creature uses to kick through the water.

Like many insects that live in the water, the common backswimmer hibernates buried in mud at the bottom of a pond. That is, it burrows into the mud during the fall and spends the winter in an inactive state. It does not become active again until late spring.

The male backswimmer tries to attract females with sounds made by scraping its legs over its mouth. The female lays its eggs soon after, attaching them to the leaves of water plants. After 20 to 30 days, the young backswimmers hatch. These young insects are called nymphs, and they look like small, wingless versions of their parents. As the nymphs grow, they shed their skin several times. Each time they shed, they add a little more wing to their bodies. Finally, in late summer, they grow full-size wings and become adult backswimmers.

Large, Short-nosed Bandicoot
Isoodon macrourus

Length of the Body: up to 19 inches
Length of the Tail: up to 7 inches
Diet: small animals, berries, seeds, and sugarcane

Weight: up to 3⅓ pounds
Number of Young: 2 to 4
Home: northern and eastern Australia
Order: Marsupials
Family: Bandicoots

  Grasslands

 Mammals

© KLEIN-HUBERT / PETER ARNOLD, INC.

The old British saying "miserable as a bandicoot" may refer to this marsupial's unpleasant disposition. Bandicoots are quite quarrelsome among themselves—so much so that, in captivity, they must be kept in separate enclosures. In the wild this creature spends much time marking its territory to warn away intruders. It does so by rubbing its scent glands against rocks and stems. This species is a nocturnal hunter that sniffs out hidden prey such as buried earthworms, insects, sleeping mice, and birds.

During breeding season, these bandicoots become sociable with the opposite sex. After mating, the male and female build a grass nest in a shallow dirt burrow or in a hollow tree stump. Just 12 days after breeding, the female gives birth to up to four tiny pups. In the first 10 minutes of life, the babies must crawl into their mother's belly pouch, or "marsupium." There they attach themselves to her nipples and nurse. Soon after the first litter is weaned, a second brood is born.

Despite their fast reproduction rate, short-nosed bandicoots are growing rare. Their problems began when European farmers came to Australia. Then, as today, the farmers extinguished the natural wildfires that kept fresh grass growing in the bandicoot's habitat. The animals need the grass as shelter for themselves and their prey.

Half-banded Barb
Capoeta semifasciolata

Length: up to 2½ inches
Home: southeastern China and Hainan Island
Number of Eggs: several hundred

Diet: plant and animal matter
Order: Carps and their relatives
Family: Carps

 Fresh Water

 Fish

© MARK SMITH / PHOTO RESEARCHERS

In southeastern China the half-banded barb is abundant in rice paddies and small, grassy irrigation reservoirs. Those kept as pets in North America are commonly golden yellow, from a variety bred in New Jersey shortly after World War II. But in the wild, this species varies greatly in color.

Because of their peaceful nature, half-banded barbs are excellent additions to aquariums filled with other fresh- and warm-water fish. They need a large, sunny tank—well planted, but with plenty of open space for swimming. They like soft, dark soil on the bottom of the tank, where they search for fallen food. Half-banded barbs have a hearty appetite and may spend the entire day snuffling through the soil.

These fish breed easily and prolifically in captivity. Generally it's a good idea to use a separate breeding tank for a spawning pair. Put the pair in their breeding tank in the evening, and place the tank near an eastern-facing window. As the first rays of morning sun hit the tank, the fish will mate. The female may start the commotion by chasing after the male. Or he may approach her with a dancing movement, darting at her side and nudging her with his open mouth. The fish then retreat to a clump of plants, where they mate. The yellow fertilized eggs stick to the plants or fall to the bottom of the tank. Be sure to separate the parents from the eggs; half-banded barbs often eat their own eggs!

Crimson-breasted Barbet
Megalaima haemacephala

Length: about 6 inches
Weight: about 1½ ounces
Diet: fruits and insects
Home: India, Sri Lanka, and southeastern Asia

Number of Eggs: 2 to 4
Order: Woodpeckers, toucans, and honeyguides
Family: Barbets

 Cities, Towns, and Farms

 Birds

© PREMAPHOTOS / ANIMALS ANIMALS / EARTH SCENES

The crimson-breasted barbet has characteristic tufts of red feathers on its chest and head. Like most barbets, this stout little bird has a large head and bill with a fringe of long whiskers. Both sexes wear the same pattern of bright colors. Like their cousins the woodpeckers, barbets have "zygodactyl" feet, which means that two toes point forward and two point backward. This enables the barbet to easily climb straight up a tree trunk or cling tightly to a swaying branch. Another similarity between woodpeckers and barbets: both have a hard, sturdy beak.

January to June is breeding season for these birds. The mated pair chisels a nest hole in a dead tree branch. After the female lays her eggs, she and her mate take turns incubating them. They also share in feeding duties after the chicks hatch. Although their original habitat was the rainforest, barbets now often nest in gardens and city parks.

Crimson-breasted barbets do not gather in flocks. Instead, they eat alone or with their mate, sometimes accompanied by their half-grown young. Like several tropical barbets, this species has a liking for figs and other soft, sweet fruits. The bird can cause trouble in orchards and plantations by eating all the crop. Crimson-breasted barbets also devour flying insects. Although their flight looks awkward, these stocky birds are agile enough to catch insects in midair.

Common Goose Barnacle
Lepas anatifera

Total Length: 6 inches
Length of the Stalk: 3 inches
Method of Reproduction:
  eggs that hatch as larvae
Home: all oceans except
  Arctic Ocean

Diet: plankton and debris
Order: Barnacles and their
  relatives
Family: Goose barnacles and
  their relatives

Oceans and
Shores

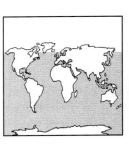

Other
Invertebrates

© NORBERT WU / MINDEN PICTURES

There's an old myth about the common goose barnacle that dates back to the Middle Ages and explains its name. Each fall in the British Isles, geese returned at the same time that barnacle-covered driftwood began washing ashore. There must be some connection, the people thought. And so the story was told that the barnacles actually developed into geese. For evidence the people pointed to the goose barnacle's feathery frill, called cirri. The fact that cirri look like feathers is, of course, just a coincidence. The truth is that geese return from their summer breeding grounds north of the Arctic Circle at about the time autumn storms begin washing driftwood ashore.

The goose barnacle's cirri look feathery because they are covered with tiny hairs.

The barnacle uses the hairs to comb tiny organisms and particles out of the water. The barnacle then pulls this food into its body and digests it. Although they usually eat only small creatures, scientists have seen the common goose barnacle grab onto bits of food much larger than itself.

The common goose barnacle can be found covering just about anything that drifts in the ocean: buoys, bottles, driftwood, boats, and even snails! Unlike the firmly attached adult, immature goose barnacles, or larvae, can swim. The larvae are attracted to the dark undersides of objects floating on the surface of the water. They attach themselves in small groups and grow hardened shells.

Pacific Barracuda
Sphyraena argentea

Length: up to 4 feet
Weight: up to 18 pounds
Diet: fish, particularly sardines
Method of Reproduction: egg layer

Home: eastern Pacific Ocean, off the coast of North America
Order: Perchlike fishes
Family: Barracudas

 Oceans and Shores

 Fish

© STEPHEN FRINK / CORBIS

The sight of a Pacific barracuda is enough to make a school of little fish flee in the opposite direction. Hunting by sight alone, the barracuda usually swims near the ocean's surface, not far from shore. There it chases sardines and other fish that travel in schools. Barracuda, especially young ones, also swim in small schools. During a typical hunting expedition, a group of barracuda may herd a school of smaller fish into shallow water. While some of the barracuda guard their victims to prevent escape, others dart into the school and grab the prey. The Pacific barracuda does not attack people. But people catch these fish and eat their tasty flesh.

The Pacific barracuda is an excellent swimmer. Its long, streamlined body is designed for racing through the sea. This fish has a long snout and a mouth that can open very wide. The mouth contains a set of large, powerful teeth, which it uses to grab prey. The upper parts of the barracuda are brownish or bluish, and the underside is silvery. This coloration provides the fish with excellent camouflage.

Pacific barracuda spend the winter off the coast of Mexico and Southern California. In spring, they move up the coast as far as Alaska to spawn. There the female releases her eggs. Many of the eggs are eaten by predators; very few hatch to eventually develop into adults.

Double-crested Basilisk
Basiliscus plumifrons

Length: 18 to 28 inches
Diet: insects, snails, fish, frogs, small lizards, fruits, and flowers
Number of Eggs: up to 20

Home: Nicaragua, Costa Rica, and Panama
Order: Lizards and snakes
Family: Iguanas

 Rainforests

 Reptiles

© STEPHEN DALTON / PHOTO RESEARCHERS

The double-crested basilisk has the remarkable ability to run across the surfaces of ponds and streams at speeds of up to 8 miles per hour! To accomplish this feat, the iguana rears up on its hind legs, using only its wide toes to briefly touch the water surface. The native people of Central America have nicknamed this species the "Jesus Christ lizard" for this ability to literally "walk on water." Basilisks also spend time on solid ground, hunting for food in trees and shrubs.

The male is recognized by a hard crest between his eyes and a second, floppier crest at the back of his head. The crests are an important part of the male's "costume" when he performs for females and tries to scare away other males. As the male displays his crests, he bobs his head, opens his mouth widely, and performs what seem to be body push-ups.

Males and females spend most of their day fighting or mating. A successful male defends the borders of his territory from many other males. Within his realm the male tries to breed with as many females as possible. Each of his mates can breed with him several times a year. After mating, the female lays a clutch of up to 20 eggs. When not occupied with the daily tasks of fighting and mating, these creatures hunt for insects, small animals, and fruits.

Gambian Epaulet Bat
Epomophorus gambianus

Length of the Body: about 6⅓ inches
Length of the Forearm: about 3⅓ inches
Weight: 3½ to 5⅓ ounces

Diet: fruits and nectar
Number of Young: 1; rarely 2
Home: central Africa
Order: Bats
Family: Old World fruit bats

 Grasslands

 Mammals

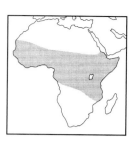

© MERLIN D. TUTTLE / PHOTO RESEARCHERS

The Gambian epaulet bat is named for the white patches on the male's shoulders. These tufts of long, bright fur reminded Europeans of the fancy shoulder pads, or epaulets, once worn by military officers. The male epaulet bat can turn his white shoulder pads inside out to form pockets. Their function remains a mystery. Perhaps they are attractive to female bats and so encourage mating. Both sexes have patches of long white fur around their ears.

The epaulet bat has a foxlike face and belongs to a group of bats called "flying foxes." Despite its sharp teeth, which could easily bite small animals, this bat is a strict vegetarian. It is particularly fond of sweet, juicy fruits such as mango and fig. It also sips nectar from the blossoms of baobab, sausage, and locust-bean trees. These flowering trees may not be able to pollinate their own blossoms without the bat's help. They grow only in regions where the epaulet bat is present.

Some epaulet bats live in the Congo rainforest, but they are more common in open woodlands and among the gallery forests of the African savanna. During the day, they sleep hanging from tree branches and bamboo stalks. Generally solitary, epaulets occasionally roost in small groups of up to 20 animals. At dusk the bats fly from their roosts and feed throughout the night.

Honduran White Bat

Ectophylla alba

Length of the Body: up to 5 inches
Length of the Tail: up to 2 inches
Weight: up to 6 ounces
Diet: insects, fruits, and nectar

Number of Young: 1
Home: Honduras, Nicaragua, and western Panama
Order: Bats
Family: American leaf-nosed bats

 Rainforests

 Mammals

© ARNOLD NEWMAN / PETER ARNOLD, INC.

White fur is quite unusual for a bat. Still there are a few white species, most notably the Honduran white bat and its cousin, the ghost bat. The Honduran variety is especially striking because its wing membranes are black, creating a dramatic contrast to its snow-white fur. Further distinguishing this species from other bats are its yellow-edged ears and nose leaf. Scientists believe that this unusual coloration makes it difficult for predators to spot the white bat in the glary tropical sunshine.

During the day, Honduran white bats roost in small groups of up to six individuals. Their roosting habits are unusual for bats, more closely resembling the nest-making behavior of birds. These bats build simple tents of banana fronds and other long, broad leaves. They carefully bite along either side of the leaf's center vein. This causes the leaf to flop down in a V shape. The bat then crawls beneath the floppy leaf for shelter.

Honduran white bats do not return to the same roost each day. Instead, they build many leafy shelters and move among them. This may confuse predators. To further avoid their enemies, white bats construct their tents six feet or more above the ground and choose leaves with long stems that hang well out from the branch. Fortunately for the bat, such long stems are too light to support the weight of a predator such as a cat, skunk, or snake.

Large Mouse-eared Bat
Myotis myotis

Length of the Body: 2¾ to 3¼ inches
Length of the Tail: about 2 inches
Diet: insects, especially moths and beetles

Weight: 0.6 to 1.6 ounces
Number of Young: 1
Home: Europe and Asia Minor
Order: Bats
Family: Evening bats

Cities, Towns, and Farms

Mammals

© GERARD LACZ / PETER ARNOLD, INC.

The large mouse-eared bat waits until night has fallen. Then it leaves its roost (resting place) and flies in search of insects along the edge of forests, across pastures, and in open woodlands. No insect is safe—the bat seizes prey in the air and on the ground.

This flying hunter does not depend on its small eyes to spot prey. Instead, it uses its excellent sense of hearing. The bat finds prey by a system called echolocation. As the bat flies, it produces sounds that reflect from objects in its path and return as echoes. With this system the large mouse-eared bat can even locate beetles rustling among grasses on the ground.

The bat's wings are well adapted to flying. Thin, lightweight finger and arm bones form the main wing structure. Skin stretches over the bones—much as fabric stretches over the metal ribs of an umbrella. At the end of each wing is a short thumb, which ends in a claw. Each back foot has five claws.

Large mouse-eared bats live in colonies that may contain thousands of individuals. They often settle under roofs or inhabit caves and mines. These creatures migrate between winter and summer roosts. Populations of large mouse-eared bats have decreased because people have destroyed their roosting sites. Unfortunately, people also hunt and kill the bats out of fear. These creatures are very helpful because they destroy many insect pests.

Sloth Bear
Melursus ursinus

Length: 5 to 6 feet
Height at the Shoulder: 2 to 3 feet
Diet: fruits and berries, ants, termites, bees, honey, and carrion

Weight: 200 to 250 pounds
Number of Young: 1 or 2
Home: India and Sri Lanka
Order: Carnivores
Family: Bears

Rainforests

Mammals

© DEWITT JONES / CORBIS

Sloth bears get their name from their long, curved claws, which greatly resemble those of true sloths. Long ago, these bears lived in many different habitats: the thornbrush jungles of India, the deserts of Thar, and the foothills of the Himalayas. But all these homes have been destroyed to make room for towns, cities, and farms. Today the last wild sloth bears live in a small area of tropical forest in Sri Lanka and eastern India.

The sloth bear uses its long claws as climbing hooks when it needs to quickly escape up a tree—for instance, when it is chased by a pack of wolves, boars, or wild dogs. Like a true sloth, the bear also uses its claws to tear open termite nests and

beehives. It can curl its long, flat tongue like a straw and suck out the tasty insects or honey inside.

A newborn sloth bear cub climbs onto its mother's back and clings to thick tufts of fur on her shoulders. It rides in this way for several weeks, climbing down only to nurse. The mother bear is very protective and will attack anything that comes near her baby—even other bears.

A sloth bear without a cub is not nearly as aggressive. Unfortunately, in its fearlessness, the sloth bear sometimes allows people to come too close. Then, if the bear suddenly feels threatened, it may slash out, inflicting terrible wounds with its daggerlike claws.

26

Eurasian Beaver
Castor fiber

Length: 31 to 43 inches
Length of the Tail: 12 to 14 inches
Diet: plants, including tree bark

Weight: 37 to 70 pounds
Number of Young: 1 to 5
Home: Europe and Asia
Order: Rodents
Family: Beavers

 Fresh Water

Mammals

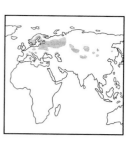

© HANS REINHARD / BRUCE COLEMAN INC.

The Eurasian beaver is one of the finest engineers in the animal kingdom. This distinction comes from the creature's ability to construct dams. These structures, sometimes 10 feet tall, block the flow of rivers and streams, creating large ponds in which the beaver builds its home, or lodge. Dam building is a family affair for beavers, although the female does most of the work. In a typical project, the beavers collect branches and debris, which they cement together using mud. Then, in the still water behind the dam, they construct their lodge, which includes an underwater entrance.

The beaver's flat, scaly tail is used as a rudder when the beaver swims. Although they breathe air, beavers can remain underwater for up to 15 minutes at a time. On land the beaver uses its tail as a support when it stands on its hind legs to gnaw trees. Beavers eat tree bark as well as thin branches and other plant matter.

The Eurasian beaver and its North American cousin are renowned for their luxurious fur. Much of the early exploration of the New World was spurred by the heavy demand for beaver pelts in Europe. The French and Indian War (1754-63) gave the British control of this lucrative industry. Although their numbers have dropped drastically, beavers are not considered endangered in any way.

Cellar Beetle
Blaps mucronata

Diet: grain (larva); dead plant and animal matter (adult)
Method of Reproduction: egg layer

Length: about 1 inch
Home: Europe
Order: Beetles
Family: Darkling beetles

 Cities, Towns, and Farms

 Arthropods

© WARWICK SLOSS / NATURE PICTURE LIBRARY

The handsome cellar beetle is most often seen at night in basements, stables, and kitchens. It is especially common in commercial kitchens, such as in hotels and bakeries, where the beetle's immature larvae, or grubs, eat flour and grain. However, these insects will eat virtually any unsealed food except meat. The beetle grub usually hides in floor cracks and other dark places. Once it matures, the beetle becomes less of a pest.

Although they were once abundant, cellar beetles have virtually disappeared from Great Britain and much of Europe. No one knows why. Perhaps they were pushed out by more successful pests such as cockroaches. Entomologists (scientists who study insects) in Britain consider this species to be "threatened." This term describes an animal that is not yet in danger of extinction, but has greatly declined in number.

Before they moved into houses and stables, cellar beetles likely lived in dry, dusty fields and desert areas. They walk very high on their "tiptoes," like people trying to avoid burning their feet on hot sand. In this position the beetles are able to cool themselves on hot, sunny days.

The cellar beetle belongs to the darkling-beetle family. It is closely related to the familiar black "stinkbug" of the American Southwest.

Checkered Beetle (Bee-wolf)
Trichodes sp.

Length: about ½ inch
Diet: insects
Method of Reproduction: egg layer

Home: North America, Europe, and Asia
Order: Beetles
Family: Checkered beetles

 Cities, Towns, and Farms

 Arthropods

© L. WEST / PHOTO RESEARCHERS

The black-and orange beetles known as bee-wolves, or checkered beetles, occasionally visit beehives to eat the residents. However, the name bee-wolf is somewhat misleading, since these predatory beetles also feed on many other kinds of insects. Other bee predators—including several species of wasp—better deserve the name.

Bee-wolves have a worse reputation than they deserve. Many adults do a service by eating the destructive larvae of wood-boring beetles. The North American bee-wolf, *T. ornatus*, also eats the pollen of cactus and yucca plants, which it helps fertilize. But the bee-wolf's grublike larvae do have a taste for young bees. Usually they eat the larvae of solitary bees, such as mason bees. Some bee-wolf larvae enter beehives. But even then they prefer to eat the dead and dying bees that fall to the bottom of the hive. Only in dirty, ill-kept hives do the larvae climb into the "nursery" to attack healthy young bees.

The adult bee-wolf's handsome markings make it a prized addition to "bug" collections. It is the adult beetle's wing covers that are so brightly colored. Rather than kill the beetle for a collection, many nature lovers prefer to gently capture it, appreciate the bee-wolf's beauty, and then let it go. Some bee-wolves are active at night and can be lured into view with lights. Others can be found inside flower blossoms.

European Rhinoceros Beetle
Oryctes nasicornis

Diet: rotting vegetation (larva); sap and nectar (adult)
Method of Reproduction: egg layer

Length: 1 to 1½ inches
Home: Europe and Asia
Order: Beetles
Family: Scarab beetles

 Cities, Towns, and Farms

 Arthropods

© DUNCAN USHER / FOTO NATURA / MINDEN PICTURES

The European rhinoceros beetle bears little resemblance to the considerably larger mammal for which it is named, except for one feature: the dramatic horn on its head. The male beetle uses its horn to joust with other males. Such duels usually conclude when one of the combatants gets knocked off a branch. Unlike its large, tropical cousins, the European rhinoceros beetle is only medium-sized, and it has adapted well to temperate climates.

European rhinoceros beetles once lived in oak forests, where they laid their eggs in the rotting bark of fallen trees. When they hatched, the large grubs, or larvae, tunneled through the soft wood, eating it as they traveled. Today most of Europe's vast, old woodlands have been cut down. Luckily, some of the beetle grubs were carried out of the forest by people who harvested the oak tree's bark. This enabled the rhinoceros beetle to move into gardens, tree nurseries, and farms. The beetle's young grubs now live in warm compost heaps and dung piles.

Rhinoceros-beetle grubs transform into winged adults in early summer and fly until the end of July. They are nocturnal insects that often flutter around lighted windows and streetlamps. Unlike the compost-chomping grubs, mature beetles drink tree sap and the juice of soft, overripe fruits. They mate on warm summer nights, and the female lays her eggs in compost heaps before dying.

Forest Dung Beetle
Geotrupes stercorarius

Length: ⅝ to 1 inch
Diet: dung
Method of Reproduction: egg layer

Home: Europe and Central Asia
Order: Beetles
Family: Scarab beetles

 Forests and Mountains

 Arthropods

© DENIS BRINGARD / PETER ARNOLD, INC.

There are about 7,000 known species of dung beetles in the world. The species of forest dung beetle that scientists call *G. stercorarius* is common in the woods of Europe. It is closely related to a North American forest dung beetle. The two species differ in one important way. In North America, forest dung beetles supplement their diet of dung, or manure, with meat scavenged from the bodies of dead animals. The European species does not.

The male and female forest dung beetle work together to build their nest. They dig a 2-foot-long tunnel straight down beneath a pile of horse manure. At the bottom of the tunnel, they hollow out a small chamber, which they fill with bits of manure. There the female lays her eggs. When they hatch, the young beetles do not look like their parents. Instead, they are plump white C-shaped grubs with very small legs. The grubs cannot fend for themselves, so their parents continue to bring new supplies of manure into the nest. Once the young beetles mature into their adult form, they leave to find mates of their own.

Although you may never see them, there can be dozens of dung beetle nests under a single manure pile. Forest dung beetles perform a valuable service as they remove manure from the forest floor. By cleaning up after other animals, dung beetles fill the last role in a food chain; they are decomposers.

Whirligig Beetle
Gyrinus sp.

Length: up to ⅓ inch
Diet: smaller water creatures
Method of Reproduction: egg layer

Home: North America, Europe, Asia, and northern Africa
Order: Beetles
Family: Whirligig beetles

 Fresh Water

 Arthropods

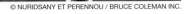
© NURIDSANY ET PERENNOU / BRUCE COLEMAN INC.

As their name implies, whirligig beetles can be delightful to watch. They gather in groups on the surface of ponds and streams, jiggling like tiny windup toys. If the whirligig "school" is disturbed, its members rush together and whirl around in tight circles.

Whirligigs are very unusual beetles for another reason: each whirligig has two pairs of eyes. The insect uses the top set to watch for ducks and other predators above the water's surface. The second set of eyes is on the underside of the beetle's head. The insect uses them to search for food and keep watch for predatory fish.

Like many water beetles, whirligigs eat fish eggs, tiny insects, and freshwater crustaceans. They can swim rapidly after prey, on the surface and underwater. Whirligigs "row" through the water using their middle and back legs, which are flattened like short paddles. The front legs are long and slender, but strong enough to capture prey.

There are two common types, or genera, of whirligigs. Those in the genus *Gyrinus* are small, no more than a third of an inch in length. This is the type of whirligig generally found in North America. Larger whirligigs belong to the genus *Dineutus* and can grow over a half inch in length. It is said that some whirligigs smell like pineapples when handled.

Greater Bird of Paradise
Paradisaea apoda

Length of the Body: 17 to 18 inches
Length of the Tail: up to 30 inches (male); 6 to 7 inches (female)
Diet: mainly fruits and insects

Number of Eggs: usually 2
Home: New Guinea and Aru islands
Order: Perching birds
Family: Birds of paradise

 Rainforests

 Birds

© PHIL SAVOIE / NATURE PICTURE LIBRARY

Europeans had their first glimpse of the greater bird of paradise in the 17th century, when traders brought back several feathered skins from Asia. The traders were told that the bird fell from Heaven, or "paradise," and that its beautiful colors were formed when it flew too close to the sun. Further suggesting a divine origin, the dead birds had no feet. "Only a bird from paradise needs no feet," the traders said. What they didn't know was that native hunters had removed the birds' feet before they skinned them. Even the scientists of Europe were fooled and named this species *Paradisaea apoda*, meaning the "legless bird of paradise."

Because males with fantastic feathers had more success attracting mates, these traits were favored in evolution. During December and January, the males gather in groups and crowd onto the branches of a large tree, where they excitedly hop from branch to branch. Every few moments a male lifts the lacy plumes on his sides to form two fantastic golden fans. He also raises his wings over his back and bends his enormous tail forward.

At the center of each group is a dominant male, who keeps the others to the outer branches. When a female appears, the dancing males all freeze on their perches. Usually she mates with the dominant male. The female builds a nest and lays two brown eggs marked with speckles. She tends the eggs and raises her chicks alone.

Bitterling
Rhodeus sericeus

Diet: larval fish, small crustaceans, and plankton
Method of Reproduction: egg layer
Home: Eurasia, Great Britain, and New York State

Length: up to 3½ inches
Order: Carps and their relatives
Family: Carps
Subfamily: Bitterlings

 Fresh Water

 Fish

© WIL MEINDERTS / FOTO NATURA / MINDEN PICTURES

All members of the genus *Rhodeus* are called bitterlings. Small-mouthed, with no teeth, these freshwater fish can feed only on very tiny animals. Bitterlings are best known for their unusual—and very clever—method of reproduction.

Between March and August, the female bitterling grows a long tube from an area on her belly. This tube, called an ovipositor, hangs into the water and stretches back nearly the length of her tail. When she is ready to lay her eggs, the female inserts the tube into the breathing siphon of a freshwater mussel. Like an underwater butterfly, the female bitterling swims from mussel to mussel, depositing a few eggs into each. Following close behind the female, one or more male bitterlings fertilize the mussels. When the mussels inhale, they suck up the bitterling's eggs and sperm into their gills. There the eggs develop, protected from harm by the mussels' hard shell. When they hatch, the baby bitterlings remain inside the mussels for a short time. After they grow into free-swimming fish, the young leave and seek shelter in weeds.

Bitterlings were introduced into both Great Britain and New York State more than 70 years ago. In 1923 someone released an aquarium full of bitterlings into the Saw Mill and Bronx rivers, near New York City. The descendants of this single introduction still thrive today.

Eurasian Bittern
Botaurus stellaris

Length: about 2½ feet
Wingspan: about 4¼ feet
Weight: about 2½ pounds
Diet: mainly fish, frogs, salamanders, and insects

Number of Eggs: 4 to 6
Home: Europe, Asia, and Africa
Order: Stilt-legged birds
Family: Herons and bitterns

Fresh Water

Birds

© DO VAN DIJCK / FOTO NATURA / MINDEN PICTURES

The Eurasian bittern is a short, chubby wading bird that greatly resembles its smaller cousin, the American bittern. Golden-brown and dappled, it is solitary and active during the day. But people rarely see it because it lives hidden among tall reeds in swamps and around lakes, ponds, and channels.

In spring the male makes a frequent, booming call. His distinctive "whooomp" is most often heard at dusk. Like a distant foghorn, the sound carries for up to a mile. From late winter through midsummer, each male defends a large territory from other males. But he allows several females to make their nests within its borders. He guards his mate from danger. But he does not care for the eggs or young because the females do not allow him to approach their nests once they have laid their eggs. The chicks clumsily follow their mother when they are about two weeks old, and they quickly learn to hunt on their own.

The Eurasian bittern finds prey while slowly wading through shallow water. After grabbing a fish with its bill, the bittern shakes or bites the prey to death. The bird catches frogs, salamanders, and mice by stabbing them through the back with its dagger-shaped beak. Occasionally bitterns even catch and eat small birds such as wrens. The young feed mainly on tadpoles and insects.

Blackbuck
Antilope cervicapra

Length: 3½ to 5 feet
Weight: 55 to 77 pounds
Diet: grasses, leaves, and other plant matter
Number of Young: 1

Home: India; introduced into Texas and Argentina
Order: Even-toed hoofed mammals
Family: Bovines

 Grasslands

 Mammals

© TOM BRAKEFIELD / BRUCE COLEMAN INC.

Whoever named the blackbuck must have thought that the species contained only males! After all, only the males (or bucks) are black, and even that color is limited just to their upper sides. The females (or does) sport a light brown coat, as do the young.

The male blackbuck has a pair of long, twisted horns. The horns are permanent; unlike a deer's antlers, they do not fall off each year. The horns are useful weapons against predators and against other male blackbucks, especially during the mating season. At that time of year, male blackbucks fight one another for possession of females, which lack horns altogether.

Blackbucks live in herds. Each adult male has his own territory, which he marks with secretions from glands on his head. He leads a herd that consists of females and young animals. When young males in the herd become adults, they are driven away. For a while the young males join together, forming "bachelor herds." Eventually each young male establishes his own territory.

Because of extensive hunting and destruction of their habitats, blackbucks are rare in their native habitat in India. Fortunately, blackbucks have adapted well to living and reproducing in zoos. Some zoo-raised blackbucks have even been introduced to Argentina and to ranches in Texas. Today there are many more blackbucks in Texas than in India!

Blue-backed Fairy Bluebird
Irena puella

Length: about 10 inches
Weight: about 2 ounces
Diet: nectar, fruits, berries, and insects
Number of Eggs: 2

Home: India, Southeast Asia, Andaman Islands, and the Philippines
Order: Perching birds
Family: Leafbirds

Forests and Mountains

Birds

Unlike most forest birds, the blue-backed fairy bluebird generally avoids meadows and woodland edges. It lives in the deepest, darkest parts of evergreen forests. As a result, the bluebirds are seldom seen except when they visit a stream to drink and bathe. The male is a special treat to glimpse, with his "cape" of brilliant blue feathers and his velvety-black face, wings, belly, and tail. His eyes are deep red. As with many bird species, the female is less striking. Her plumage is a dull blue with black trim.

Like a storybook fairy, this bluebird constantly flits and hops while it darts among high branches and treetops. As it flutters about, it whistles a bubbly song: "wheet-wheet-wheet-wheet," or "be-quick, be-quick, be-quick." In flight it chatters with a sharp-sounding "chichichichik!" Fairy bluebirds love sweets and feed mainly on figs and the nectar of erythrina and grevillea trees.

Blue-backed fairy bluebirds mate and raise their families from January to June. The female does all the nest building, but her mate keeps her company and constantly serenades her. The female places her nest securely in the fork of a shady tree or bush, about 15 feet above the ground. It is a unique nest, made out of thick sticks and assembled into a sturdy platform about the size of a dinner plate. The female bluebird incubates the eggs, but both parents share the task of feeding the chicks.

Blue-footed Booby
Sula nebouxii

Length: 29 to 32 inches
Weight: about 4 pounds (female); about 2¾ pounds (male)
Diet: mainly fish and squid

Number of Eggs: 2
Home: eastern Pacific Ocean
Order: Pelicans and gannets
Family: Gannets and boobies

  Oceans and Shores

 Birds

© WOLFGANG KAEHLER / CORBIS

The blue-footed booby is easily recognized by its brightly colored, webbed feet. Like other boobies, this species has a heavy, torpedo-shaped body designed for plunging into the ocean. These birds have the unusual habit of hunting in organized flocks. Hovering over a school of fish, the group waits to dive at exactly the same time—on the squawk of one member. By diving together, the boobies block the escape of fish that would otherwise slip away. Bluefoots are the only species of booby to feed cooperatively in this way.

In the breeding season, blue-footed boobies gather in large colonies on the Galápagos Islands; along the coasts of Peru, Colombia, and Panama; and in the Gulf of California. These breeding sites are all near a rich fishing area—the Peru Current. This deep, cool current of water sweeps nutrients up to the surface of the Pacific Ocean, producing an abundance of fish and other food. Because they are so well-fed, blue-footed boobies are able to raise two chicks at a time. In comparison, other booby species have only enough food for, at most, one chick a year. When fishing is particularly good, Galápagos bluefoots may in a single season lay a second clutch of eggs.

According to folklore, boobies are named for their habit of landing on sailing ships and "stupidly" allowing sailors to kill them. Boobies still seem to enjoy following ships—perhaps only out of curiosity.

Brown Booby
Sula leucogaster

Length: 25 to 29 inches
Weight: up to 8 pounds
Home: tropical waters of the Atlantic, Pacific, and Indian oceans

Diet: fish and squid
Number of Eggs: 1 or 2
Order: Pelicans and gannets
Family: Boobies

Oceans and Shores

Birds

© KEVIN SCHAEFER / CORBIS

Boobies are exceptionally tame and often visit ships passing through tropical waters. Old-time sailors named them "boobies" because the birds were foolish enough to allow men to approach and kill them. As a result, these birds were often served for dinner when other ship supplies were scarce.

While most species of booby fly over the open ocean, the brown booby stays close to shore. It nests on cliffs, rocky beaches, and the occasional coral reef. The female scrapes a crude nest in the dirt or simply lays her eggs on a hard rock or coral. Both parents share in warming the eggs and then feeding their young. They take turns flying back to the sea to catch squid and fish. After swallowing prey, the parent booby flies home and coughs up the food for its chick or chicks. Sometimes a brown booby with a stomach full of food for its family is robbed of the meal. Great frigatebirds will gang up on a booby, pestering the poor bird until it coughs up some fish or squid.

Like all boobies, this species hunts by looking down through the water as it flies. When it spies a school of fish or squid, the bird plunges straight down into the ocean. Brown boobies prefer to hunt over clear, shallow water, where fish are most visible. They are especially abundant on Kauai, one of the Hawaiian Islands.

Satin Bower-bird
Ptilonorhynchus violaceus

Length: 10 to 15 inches
Diet: fruits, berries, and insects
Number of Eggs: 2
Home: eastern Australia

Order: Perching birds
Family: Birds of paradise and bower birds

Rainforests

Birds

© PAM GARDNER / FRANK LANE PICTURE AGENCY / CORBIS

Most birds build a nest only when it's time to lay eggs. The male satin bower-bird of eastern Australia, however, spends his entire life building an intricate courtship dwelling called a bower. The stick shelter is built in the shape of a long passageway. One end of the passageway opens onto a platform lined with all sorts of items, including flowers, bits of plastic, and glass. Satin bower-birds are attracted to shiny blue decorations, and much of the bower is strewn with blue bottle caps, buttons, and yarn.

Early each morning the male flies down to the bower from his roost high in the trees. He busily tidies up the shelter and its platform, and then makes several trips in search of new trinkets. He does this in preparation for female visitors. When the female visits the male's dwelling, she is presented with one of his favorite possessions—usually a bright-blue object—that he carries to her in his beak. He excitedly jumps about on the display platform. As he dances, he puffs out his feathers, flaps his wings, and sings a noisy melody full of whistles, hisses, and clicks.

After mating, the female quickly leaves, while the male stays behind and prepares for the arrival of another mate. Working alone, the female weaves a nest of twigs and leaves at the top of a tree. She incubates her eggs and raises the chicks with no help from her mate.

Bowfin
Amia calva

Length: up to 25 inches
Weight: up to 8 pounds
Diet: fish
Home: eastern United States

Method of Reproduction: egg layer
Order: Bowfins
Family: Bowfins

 Fresh Water

 Fish

© TOM MCHUGH / PHOTO RESEARCHERS

Bowfins live in lakes and slow-moving rivers east of the Rocky Mountains in the United States. During warm weather, they live in shallow, weed-filled areas, sometimes coming to the surface to gulp air. In winter, they move to deeper water. Packed together in large groups, the bowfins rest during the cold weather. When spring arrives and temperatures rise, they return to the shallow water.

Spring is also mating season. The males become brightly colored, with touches of yellow, bronze, and bright green. Each male bowfin builds a circular nest among the weeds. He uses his mouth to remove plants from the bottom, then uses his fins to clear away silt. He gathers roots to form the nest.

After a while a female approaches, and the two fish court. As the female lays her eggs, the male fertilizes them. The female leaves, but the male stays nearby. He removes mud that settles on the eggs, and he chases away other fish that try to feed on the eggs. The male also protects the young fish after they hatch. When the young are big enough to leave their nest, they usually stay together in a group, or school. The school swims under the father as he moves through the water. If predators approach, the father hits them with his tail and shoves them out of the way. Young bowfins eat mostly invertebrates. As they get older, their diet changes to fish.

Common Bream
Abramis brama

Length: 12 to 20 inches
Diet: insects, worms, mollusks, and plants
Method of Reproduction: egg layer

Weight: 8 to 9 pounds
Home: Europe
Order: Carps and their relatives
Family: Minnows

 Fresh Water

 Fish

© CLAUDE GUIHARD / PETER ARNOLD, INC.

The common bream is a popular food fish in Europe, especially in eastern Europe, where it is caught commercially. A large bream is said to be as tasty as a carp. But small ones are too bony to eat. A lively fish, the common bream is popular with sports fishermen as well.

These humpbacked fish are very slender and slimy to the touch. Newborn bream are white, but they darken to a greenish or brownish hue as adults. A young common bream is ready to mate when it is four years old and about a foot long. The breeding male develops warts and bumps on his body. He uses these "nuptial tubercles" to stroke the female prior to mating.

Bream that live in large rivers migrate long distances to a spawning site, usually the same place where they were born. Bream in ponds and small rivers simply gather in shallow water a day or two before they are ready to mate.

With much splashing, leaping, and rolling, each male tries to defend a small territory. The successful male is able to entice a female to shed her sticky yellow eggs in his turf. She deposits the eggs while rubbing against weeds and other plant matter. The eggs stick to the leaves. The male then fertilizes the eggs. After mating, the bream return to deep water, leaving their eggs to hatch in about 10 days.

Red Brocket
Mazama americana

Length: 2½ to 4½ feet
Height at the Shoulder: about 2 feet
Weight: 35 to 55 pounds
Diet: leaves, grasses, and fruits

Number of Young: 1
Home: Central and South America
Order: Even-toed hoofed mammals
Family: Deer

  Rainforests

Mammals

© KEVIN SCHAFER / CORBIS

As a group, brockets include four species of small deer that live in Central and South America. *Brocket* is an Old French word meaning "the spike of an antler." Each of the male's antlers consists of just a single short spike, unlike the many-branched antlers of North American and European deer.

The red brocket, named for the color of its rusty coat, is the most common and familiar of its kind. This species is very shy. During the day, it sleeps in the rainforest, hidden beneath fallen logs or in the crevices between large tree roots. In the evening the brocket may slip quietly into nearby plantations or vegetable gardens to eat. The deer lives a solitary life within its personal territory. To mark its boundaries, it rubs a scented gland located on the forehead against trees, rocks, and other objects. The scent warns other brockets to stay away.

Unlike deer in North America and Europe, brockets do not breed during a particular season, although a large number of fawns are born during the winter dry season (July through September). When a doe is ready to mate, she enters the territory of a neighboring male for a brief visit. She gives birth about six months later. The fawn's speckled coat is excellent camouflage in the forest underbrush. Family time is brief, however. The doe weans her fawn in as little as a few weeks, and they separate permanently six months later. Red brockets can live up to 12 years.

Water Buffalo
Bubalus bubalis

Length of the Body: 8 to 9¼ feet
Length of the Tail: 2 to 2¾ feet
Height at the Shoulder: 5¼ to 6¼ feet
Weight: 1,750 to 2,650 pounds

Diet: plants
Number of Young: 1
Home: Southeast Asia
Order: Even-toed hoofed mammals
Family: Bovines

 Fresh Water

 Mammals

The water buffalo has quite an interesting method of protecting itself from flies and other pesky insects. First it finds just the right watering hole. Then the buffalo rolls around in the hole, covering its entire body with a thick layer of mud. When the mud dries, it forms a hard crust that insects cannot penetrate. If the buffalo comes across a lake or river, it may submerge its body until only its nostrils are above the water's surface. This also protects the animal from insect bites.

The water buffalo is a large, powerful animal with curved horns that may grow to a length of more than six feet. The creature's long, broad hooves are useful for walking over soggy ground in swamps and other wetlands. Grass and plants growing in or alongside these watery habitats are the buffalo's main source of food.

The water buffalo, although not endangered, is quite rare in the wild. However, people have domesticated this animal for use as a source of milk, to till rice fields, and as a draft animal (to pull loads). Millions of domesticated water buffalo live in Asia and other parts of the world.

In the wild, each male gathers a harem (group) of females during the mating season. A female is pregnant for about 10 months and usually gives birth to a single calf. The water buffalo has a life span of about 20 years.

Set Index